Your friend in Christ,

Teri Lynn

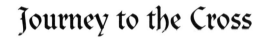

Journey to the Cross

Journey to the Cross

A Lenten Devotional

Teri Lynn

1998
Galde Press, Inc.
Lakeville, Minnesota, U.S.A.

First Edition
First Printing, 1998

ISBN 1–880090–71–6

Galde Press, Inc.
PO Box 460
Lakeville, Minnesota 55044–0460

Where Did Lent Come From?

Actually, it's the word *Lenten* which comes from the word "lengthen," or that time of the year when the days start to get longer. The German word for Lent is *Fastenzeit*, or "fasting time," traditionally that time when we lose our winter weight by fasting and praying.

Spring is also the time to sweep the grit out of our garages and clean out the basement. Why should it be any different with our souls? As we open the windows of our homes to let out the stuffy, dry winter air, we let the warmer moist breezes of springtime freshen up our houses. So also we let the Holy Spirit blow his fresh wind through our souls.

Christians first started celebrating Lent over 1,500 years ago as a *quarantine* before Easter. Quarantine is nothing more and nothing less than the Latin word for "forty." Medicine has borrowed this word from the church. New converts were quarantines or locked out of the church for forty days to think it over before submitting to Baptism on Easter.

Once infant baptism took hold as the norm, there were fewer and fewer converts to go through the quarantine, and it became a general time for spiritual refocus; complete with fasting and praying.

Several traditions emphasize Lent, none more richly than Lutherans, who tend to have midweek services, sing hymns in a minor key, and ban most frivolity from the church building for forty days.

America, with its Bible-centered Protestantism as the norm, emphasizes Lent less than do the immigrant churches (Catholics, Lutherans, etc.) from Europe in its midst. However, surrounded by an ever louder and busier society, the call to quietness, simplicity, and discipline are needed now perhaps more than ever.

—Dave Housholder
with Bill Bohline

Pastors
Hosanna!
Lakevile, Minensota

The period of forty days from Ash Wednesday to Easter, observed variously in Christian churches by fasting and penitence, is the dictionary term for Lent.

As your Lenten journey begins, make it a positive experience on your way to the cross. Let Christ's suffering pave the way for you as you learn more about His Word.

Each one of us is a tender, loving jewel formed in the image of God. Some of us have more sparkle and shine, while some of us are still a little rough on the edges. Each one of us possesses the ability to become a beautiful gem if we work daily on some of the rough edges.

Journey daily through Lent and share from God's Word as He brings to you daily a new experience.

Let the journey begin!

Matthew 5: 3-16

3 *"Blessed are the poor in spirit, for theirs is the kingdom of heaven.*

4 *"Blessed are those who mourn, for they shall be comforted.*

5 *"Blessed are the meek, for they shall inherit the earth.*

6 *"Blessed are those who hunger and thirst for righteousness, for they shall be satisfied.*

7 *"Blessed are the merciful, for they shall obtain mercy.*

8 *"Blessed are the pure in heart, for they shall see God.*

9 *"Blessed are the peacemakers, for they shall be called sons of God.*

10 *"Blessed are those who are persecuted for righteousness' sake, for theirs is the kingdom of heaven.*

11 *"Blessed are you when men revile you and persecute you and utter all kinds of evil against you falsely on my account.*

12 *"Rejoice and be glad, for your reward is great in heaven, for so men persecuted the prophets who were before you.*

13 *"You are the salt of the earth: but if salt has lost its taste, how shall its saltness be restored? It is no longer good for anything except to be thrown out and trodden under foot by men.*

14 *"You are the light of the world. A city set on a hill cannot be hid* [15] *Nor do men light a lamp and put it under a bushel, but on a stand, and it gives light to all in the house.* [16] *Let your light so shine before men, that they may see your good works and give glory to your Father who is in heaven."*

Day 1 — Ash Wednesday

Food for Thought

Begin your Lenten Journey with a very positive step. Take the time to list some positive qualities about yourself. Think of the characteristics that others have pointed out to you: patience, endurance, gentleness, good listener, kind, thoughtful, disciplined, etc.

Now that you have made your list, concentrate on these qualities you are blessed with. Thank God for each quality and for how He has blessed you. Do not ever take for granted your blessings.

There are many who have handicaps, who may not hear, see, walk or talk. These are frequently things we seldom give thanks for but often take for granted. Take what God has given you and use it this day for His glory.

Prayer

Thank You, Lord, for the gifts You have given to me.
Never let me abuse them or get so used to them that I take
them for granted.

Amen

2 Peter 1:3-15

3 His divine power has granted to us all things that pertain to life and godliness, through the knowledge of him who called us to his own glory and excellence ⁴by which he has granted to us his precious and very great promises, that through these you may escape from the corruption that is in the world because of passion, and become partakers of the divine nature. ⁵For this very reason make every effort to supplement your faith with virtue, and virtue with knowledge, ⁶and knowledge with self-control, and self-control with steadfastness, and steadfastness with godliness, ⁷and godliness with brotherly love. ⁸For if these things are yours and abound, they keep you from being ineffective or unfruitful in the knowledge of our Lord Jesus Christ. ⁹For whoever lacks these things is blind and shortsighted and has forgotten that he was cleansed from his old sins. ¹⁰Therefore, brethren, be the more zealous to confirm your call and election, for if you do this you will never fall; ¹¹so there will be richly provided for you an entrance into the eternal kingdom of our Lord and Savior Jesus Christ.

12 Therefore I intend always to remind you of these things, though you know them and are established in the truth that you have. ¹³I think it right, as long as I am in this body, to arouse you by way of reminder, ¹⁴since I know that the putting off of my body will be soon, as our Lord Jesus Christ showed me. ¹⁵And I will see to it that after my departure you may be able at any time to recall these things.

Day 2, Thursday — Routine

Food for Thought

Have you ever had one of those mornings when you wish you had stayed in bed? Often times those mornings might coincide with Monday mornings. Why is it that after a weekend of "R & R" it is so hard to drag oneself out of bed on Monday morning? Is it the routine we don't want to face? Think about routine and how little would be accomplished without it. We all need patterns and routine in our lives.

Many times a lack of routine is a sign of distress. Something has gone wrong. Sometimes it is a needed diversion to get away from it all. Whatever the reason, it is always good to get back to the routine.

Routine keeps us on schedule and helps us accomplish goals. Set a goal today to accomplish something good for someone else. Be thankful that we have routine. Make it a part of your routine to talk to God daily and read from His Word. It will be a brighter day whatever comes your way.

Prayer

Thank You, God, for routine that keeps us on track. Help me to keep in constant routine with You so that I might grow in Your grace and knowledge.

Amen

1 Samuel 16:7

7 But the Lord said to Samuel, "Do not look on his appearance or on the height of his stature, because I have rejected him; for the Lord sees not as man sees; man looks on the outward appearance, but the Lord looks on the heart."

Day 3, Friday — Divine Insight

Food for Thought

How keen are your skills at seeing? Do you use your sight to see the surface of things or to search deep into the beauty of those around us?

Getting oneself ready in the morning requires quite a routine. We all try hard to look our best. Some mornings we seem to turn out better than others. It brings great assurance to know that God has divine insight. It does not matter what our outer appearance looks like because God looks at the condition of our hearts. God does not care if we are staying in style. He cares about our attitude and how much we show our love for each other.

Throughout the day today try to sharpen your insight. Do not look at the clothes others are wearing; look into their eyes. Do you feel the pain or sense the joy they are bearing? Let others know you care. Only God has divine insight, but we can always keep fine tuning the condition of our hearts.

Prayer

Dear God, I am so grateful for your insight. Help me to sharpen my insight to those around me. Help me to concentrate on the condition of my heart more than my outward appearance.

Amen

Matthew 7:24-27

24 "Every one then who hears these words of mine and does them will be like a wise man who built his house upon the rock; 25 and the rain fell, and the floods came, and the winds blew and beat upon that house, but it did not fall, because it had been founded on the rock. 26 And every one who hears these words of mine and does not do them will be like a foolish man who built his house upon the sand; 27 and the rain fell, and the floods came, and the winds blew and beat against that house, and it fell; and great was the fall of it."

Day 4, Saturday — A Solid Foundation

Food for Thought

Is your life a little topsy-turvy? Have you checked out your foundation recently?

God gives us the example of a house built on a rock rather than sand. A house with a firm foundation can withstand much more than the house built on sand.

Christ is our solid rock. He will always be there whatever our situation. Focus on Christ and get well grounded in the Word. When the storms of life hit don't let your foundation be washed away like sand. Make sure your foundation is based on Jesus Christ, "The Rock."

Prayer

Dear Lord, I am so grateful my foundation is with You. Help me to depend on You to get me through the storms that come my way.

Amen

John 12:44-50

44 And Jesus cried out and said, "He who believes in me, believes not in me but in him who sent me. 45 And he who sees me sees him who sent me. 46 I have come as light into the world, that whoever believes in me may not remain in darkness. 47 If any one hears my sayings and does not keep them, I do not judge him; for I did not come to judge the world but to save the world. 48 He who rejects me and does not receive my sayings has a judge; the word that I have spoken will be his judge on the last day. 49 For I have not spoken on my own authority; the Father who sent me has himself given me commandment what to say and what to speak. 50 And I know that his commandment is eternal life. What I say, therefore, I say as the Father has bidden me."

First Sunday in Lent

Christ has come so we might have life.

Romans 12:3-13

3 *For by the grace given to me I bid every one among you not to think
of himself more highly than he ought to think, but to think with
sober judgment, each according to the measure of faith which God
has assigned him.* [4] *For as in one body we have many members, and
all the members do not have the same function,* [5] *so we, though
many, are one body in Christ, and individually members one of
another.* [6] *Having gifts that differ according to the grace given to us,
let us use them: if prophecy, in proportion to our faith;* [7] *if service, in
our serving; he who teaches, in his teaching;* [8] *he who exhorts, in his
exhortation; he who contributes, in liberality; he who gives aid, with
zeal; he who does acts of mercy, with cheerfulness.*

9 *Let love be genuine; hate what is evil, hold fast to what is good;* [10] *love
one another with brotherly affection; outdo one another in showing
honor.* [11] *Never flag in zeal, be aglow with the Spirit, serve the Lord.*
[12] *Rejoice in your hope, be patient in tribulation, be constant in
prayer.* [13] *Contribute to the needs of the saints, practice hospitality.*

Day 5, Monday — Ordinary People

Food for Thought

If you consider yourself an ordinary person think about this: The plain, ordinary people far outnumber the extraordinary people. It is through the ordinary people that God is able to take care of this world.

God can use us in so many ways. He can use us to comfort those struck with disaster. He uses us to provide food and shelter for the homeless. He uses us to welcome a new neighbor into the community or to be a sounding board for someone who is hurting. God uses us to care for His flock. We may be just ordinary people, yet we have a magnificent tender shepherd who counts on each one of us to do our part for Him.

To God we are the extraordinary. Let God use you this day to tend to someone in need. Be open to His voice.

Prayer

Lord, we often get so wrapped up in our own world that we forget those around us. Help me to do my part to help others in need.

Amen

1 John 2:28-29

28 And now, little children, abide in him, so that when he appears we may have confidence and not shrink from him in shame at his coming. [29] If you know that he is righteous, you may be sure that every one who does right is born of him.

Day 6, Tuesday — Angel Visits

Food for Thought

If an angel were to visit you, or even God himself, would your home be ready for this visit from this friend? Would you suddenly change the channel of your TV set? Would magazines be covered by a dusty Bible from a shelf? Would a novel you might be reading be suddenly swept under the bed? Would your radio be singing Christian lyrics with words of encouragement to those needing to be fed?

If your house would undergo some changes, it's time to stop and reflect. What is it our lives are saying about the way we live? Are we in tune to God and what His Word says. Do we try to set good examples to our children and our friends?

How would you be standing if you were entertaining this special friend?

Prayer

Lord, Help my life and my home to be a reflection of Your love and Your standards. Help me to be ready for a visit from a friend.

Amen

Proverbs 3:5-7

5 *Trust in the Lord with all your heart, and do not rely on your own insight.*

6 *In all your ways acknowledge him, and he will make straight your paths.*

7 *Be not wise in your own eyes; fear the Lord, and turn away from evil.*

Day 7, Wednesday — A Fork in the Road

Food for Thought

While wandering aimlessly down a country road, enjoying the fresh spring air, I came to a fork in the road and I didn't know which way to turn. I had lost my sense of direction, because my thoughts were on other things. If I went the wrong way, darkness might come before I arrived home. If I chose the right way, I would be home before too long. Which way would I go? It was my choice.

God has given each one of us a free will. We also have a choice of which path we will follow. Some may choose the way that looks most enticing, the way that looks easiest and offers the most fun down the path. At the end of that enticing path they will be left with nothing.

The other path may not look quite so easy. It may have hills and have more bumps along the way. It might even be gravel as opposed to paved. Along this path there is a constant compass that will always show the way. Place your hand in His hand, and He will lead you the right way. If you should fall off the path along the way just reach up. His hand will never go away.

Prayer

Dear Jesus, I picture a little child and a parent walking hand in hand. The child is holding on, trusting in that mom or dad. May this picture be You and I, Lord. Help me to never let go of Your hand.

Amen

Romans 5:6-11

6 While we were yet helpless, at the right time Christ died for the ungodly.

7 Why, one will hardly die for a righteous man—though perhaps for a good man one will even dare to die. ⁸ But God shows his love for us in that while we were yet sinners Christ died for us. ⁹ Since, therefore, we are now justified by his blood, much more shall we be saved by him from the wrath of God. ¹⁰ For if while we were enemies we were reconciled to God by the death of his Son, much more, now that we are reconciled, shall we be saved by his life. ¹¹ Not only so, but we also rejoice in God through our Lord Jesus Christ, through whom we have now received our reconciliation.

Day 8, Thursday — Unconditional Love

Food for Thought

Almost everyone at some point in time has signed a contract. If you read the contract thoroughly you will find that it is full of many areas of fine print. There are many conditions to safeguard the owner of the contract.

The Bible is full of words, but you do not have to look for the fine print. When we read God's Word we find that His love is unconditional.

Whatever has happened in your past can be forgiven and left behind. We have a future because of God's unconditional love. When you read His Word don't look for the fine print; there are no catches in this contract.

Prayer

Lord, I often wonder if I'm worthy of such love. It brings me comfort to know that whatever I've done, You can still love me and you always will. Help me to be accepting of Your unconditional love.

Amen

Psalm 42:8-11

8 By day the Lord commands his steadfast love;
   and at night his song is with me,
   and a prayer to the God of my life.

9 I say to God, my rock:
   "Why hast thou forgotten me?
   Why go I mourning
   because of the oppression of the enemy?"

10 As with a deadly wound in my body,
   my adversaries taunt me,
   while they say to me continually,
   "Where is your God?"

11 Why are you cast down, O my soul,
   and why are you disquieted within me?
   Hope in God; for I shall again praise him,
   my help and my God.

Day 9, Friday — Emergency Flashers

Food for Thought

Imagine yourself driving along on the highway when suddenly an indicator light starts flashing on your car. You may be short on time and hesitate to pull off the road. The light stays on, so you give in and pull over. One of the first things you do is turn on your emergency flashers. You turn them on to alert other cars of your car on the side of the road and to attract attention for help.

Many of us in our day-to-day living skate along quite smoothly until suddenly something happens and a tragedy of some sort might occur. Invariably we turn on our flashers and start shooting prayers upward. We many times say "why" or wonder where God was when it happened. The truth is, God was right there next to us feeling the tragedy with us. Life had been going so well that we forgot to notice. Do not take God for granted. Do not just use Him for emergencies. Use Him for everyday living. If you are in constant companionship with Him, the emergencies of life will be easier to handle. They still won't be painless and they will still come our way, but you will not feel quite so lost if you have kept God by your side day to day.

Prayer

Dear God, Help me not to forget that when life is going easy I should stay in constant fellowship with You. It is during those times that I can be so thankful and sing Your praises. Then when the storms of life hit I won't have to wonder where You are because You will be right by my side.

Amen

Matthew 8:10-13

10 When Jesus heard him, he marveled, and said to those who followed him, "Truly, I say to you, not even in Israel have I found such faith.

11 I tell you, many will come from east and west and sit at table with Abraham, Isaac, and Jacob in the kingdom of heaven, ¹² while the sons of the kingdom will be thrown into the outer darkness; there men will weep and gnash their teeth." ¹³ And to the centurion Jesus said, "God; be it done for you as you have believed." And the servant was healed at that very moment.

Day 10, Saturday — The Great Physician

Food for Thought

Have you been finding a replacement for God? Has life's corruption invaded you without even knowing?

This world offers so many false cures for depression and troubles that we face. The world has pills and drugs, shrinks and books from A-Z. There are so many false cures being represented.

Some cures may help; they may offer temporary relief or they may make you high. They can offer practical advice, but there is no better cure than within the hands of the Great Physician. He can give us comfort from distress, He can wipe the tears from our eyes. He may do this through others who are devoted to being His helpers.

Let the Father be the cure for all your needs. There is no replacement for the greatest physician of all times.

Prayer

Lord, Help me to sense Your healing powers. Help me to look to You for my source of strength. May I be open to those to whom You may entrust with my care.

Amen

John 5:19-24

19. Jesus said to them, "Truly, truly, I say to you, the Son can do nothing of his own accord, but only what he sees the Father doing; for whatever he does, that the Son does likewise. 20 For the Father loves the Son, and shows him all that he himself is doing; and greater works than these will he show him, that you may marvel. 21 For as the Father raises the dead and gives them life, so also the Son gives life to whom he will. 22 The Father judges no one, but has given all judgment to the Son, 23 that all may honor the Son, even as they honor the Father. He who does not honor the Son does not honor the Father who sent him. 24 Truly, truly, I say to you, he who hears my word and believes him who sent me, has eternal life; he does not come into judgment, but has passed from death to life.

Second Sunday in Lent

Be in tune to God's marvelous works.

Hebrews 3:7-12

7 Therefore, as the Holy Spirit says, "Today, when you hear his voice,
^{8} do not harden your hearts as in the rebellion, on the day of testing
in the wilderness, ^{9} where your fathers put me to the test and saw my
works for forty years. ^{10} Therefore I was provoked with that generation, and said, 'They always go astray in their hearts; they have not
known my ways.' ^{11} As I swore in my wrath, 'They shall never enter
my rest.' " ^{12} Take care, brethren, lest there be in any of you an evil,
unbelieving heart, leading you to fall away from the living God.

Day 11, Monday — Seek the Lord

Food for Thought

Are you taking the time to listen to the Lord? Sometimes we get so wrapped up in ourselves and those around us that we do not take the time to stop and listen and feel His presence. The Lord desires to be close to us, to offer us comfort, give us wisdom and answer our prayers. How can we receive all that if we do not stop for one-on-one quality time?

The Lord may be calling you today to offer you one of His precious gifts. Take the time to listen to His calling. Do not harden your heart to his voice.

Prayer

Lord, Fill me with the presence of Your Holy Spirit. Help me to take the time so we can have special, one-on-one quality time.

Amen

Philippians 2:14-16

14 Do all things without grumbling or questioning, [15] that you may be blameless and innocent, children of God without blemish in the midst of a crooked and perverse generation, among whom you shine as lights in the world, [16] holding fast the word of life, so that in the day of Christ I may be proud that I did not run in vain or labor in vain.

Day 12, Tuesday —
Blessed Are the Children

Food for Thought

One day while enjoying the company of a little toddler at a mall I could see why God so often refers to children in the Bible. There is nothing like the smile and innocence on the face of a little one. They are not only content with themselves, but they also create change in the expressions of all those they encounter. They seem to make even the grumpiest person smile and sometimes they even make strange expressions or noises just to see a toddler laugh. It is within little children that we can see such a beautiful life. They have not become hardened or judgmental toward others. They will smile at most anyone whether they know them or not. They are content to be taken care of and to not do everything on their own.

We are to come to Christ as little children. He loves us and wants us to let Him take care of us. Give your burdens to Him. Lighten your load and smile at someone you might not even know.

Prayer

Dear Jesus, help me to come to You as a little child who needs constant care. Help me to depend on You for all my needs. Thank You for the gift we can see in the lives of little children.

Amen

2 Corinthians 4:7-12

7 But we have this treasure in earthen vessels, to show that the transcendent power belongs to God and not to us. ⁸ We are afflicted in every way, but not crushed; perplexed, but not driven to despair; ⁹ persecuted, but not forsaken; struck down, but not destroyed; ¹⁰ always carrying in the body the death of Jesus, so that the life of Jesus may also be manifested in our bodies. ¹¹ For while we live we are always being given up to death for Jesus' sake, so that the life of Jesus may be manifested in our mortal flesh. ¹² So death is at work in us, but life in you.

Day 13, Wednesday — Out of Control

Food for Thought

Have you ever been driving on a blustery winter day and hit a patch of ice? Panic overcomes and the adrenaline starts flowing. You have little control and braking would only cause you to slide more. It is in those times of panic that we pray that God will be in control and keep us safely on the road.

God wants to be in the driver's seat of our lives. He does not want to be there only in times of panic. He wants to be there constantly. He wants us to give Him the control and to let Him take care of us even when we are not out of control.

Prayer

Lord, Help me to let You be the leader of my life. Help me to give You constant control and not just when in a panic.

Amen

Genesis 1:29-31

29 And God said, "Behold I have given you every plant yielding seed
which is upon the face of all the earth, and every tree with seed in its
fruit; you shall have them for food. 30 And to every beast of the earth,
and to every bird of the air, and to everything that creeps on the
earth, everything that has the breath of life, I have given every green
plant for food." And it was so. 31 And God saw everything that he
had made, and behold, it was very good. And there was evening and
there was morning, a sixth day.

Day 14, Thursday —
For the Beauty of the Earth

Food for Thought

What a beautiful creation we have been blessed with. Here in Minnesota we have the variety of four seasons. With each season we see a new miracle appear. In spring we see buds, fresh and fragile in nature. In summer we see the beautiful flowers in full bloom and bushy green trees. In the fall we have rainbows of color that shimmer in the crisp, cool air. In winter we see the formation of a tiny perfect flake, white and pure, no two that are alike. God's beautiful creation is all around us and yet we take it for granted.

We fill the beautiful blue sky with pollution. We are filling our land with garbage. In the midst of all out technology we are choking out His creation.

Take some time to care for God's creation. He has given it to us to tend to, not to destroy. Do something today to help restore its beauty.

Prayer

Lord, we can raise buildings to the sky, we send rockets to the moon, and we have high class technology. Help us with all our knowledge to find the cures for what we are doing to this beautiful creation.

Amen

Proverbs 14:29-33

29 *He who is slow to anger has great understanding,*
   but he who has a hasty temper exalts folly.

30 *A tranquil mind gives life to the flesh*
   but passion makes the bones rot.

31 *He who oppresses a poor man insults his Maker,*
   but he who is kind to the needy honors him.

32 *The wicked is overthrown through his evil-doing,*
   but the righteous finds refuge through his integrity.

33 *Wisdom abides in the mind of a man of understanding,*
   but it is not known in the heart of fools.

Day 15, Friday—
Irritations Heaven Bound

Food for Thought

A source of great irritation was following me down the road one day. The driver of the vehicle behind me was very close behind me. I could plainly see him, well enough to identify him in a lineup, if necessary. The driver obviously was in a great hurry.

My first reaction was anger and irritation against this person that I knew nothing about. I decided to turn my anger heavenward. I prayed for this person and for whatever troubles he might be facing. I prayed for his safety that he would not get into an accident. My irritation was turned into peace and caring for a person I did not even know.

Next time you are facing irritations, turn them heavenward. You will find yourself caring about a total stranger who was becoming your enemy.

Prayer

Dear Lord, help me to be slow to anger. Help me not to turn petty things into irritations. Forgive me for the needless anger I sometimes feel.

Amen

Proverbs 8:32-36

32 *And now, my sons, listen to me:*
  happy are those who keep my ways.

33 *Hear instruction and be wise, and do not neglect it.*

34 *Happy is the man who listens to me,*
  watching daily at my gates,
  waiting beside my doors.

35 *For he who finds me finds life*
  and obtains favor from the Lord;

36 *but he who misses me injures himself;*
  all who hate me love death."

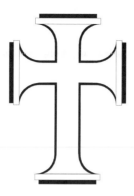

Day 16, Saturday —
"Different Strokes for Different Folks"

Food for Thought

"Different strokes for different folks" is a phrase I am sure everyone has heard before. It really is a true phrase. We are all different and we all have different things we enjoy.

There is one stroke that most everyone in life searches for, and that is happiness. Many try to find happiness in many different ways.

There is one source of true, lasting happiness in this life and that is Jesus Christ. He is the one stroke we could all have in common to find true happiness in life.

If you have not committed your life to Christ, you may still be searching. Your search can end today in accepting Christ as your Savior and committing your life to Him. We may all be different, which makes this world an interesting place, but we have one common denominator in Christ.

Prayer

Lord, I am thankful that each one of us has been made unique, yet we all have the same opportunity to find lasting happiness in Christ. Thank You for Your free gift of salvation.

Amen

John 5:25-29

25 "Truly, truly, I say to you, the hour is coming, and now is, when the dead will hear the voice of the Son of God, and those who hear will live. [26] For as the Father has life in himself, so he has granted the Son also to have life in himself, [27] and has given him authority to execute judgment, because he is the Son of man. [28] Do not marvel at this; for the hour is coming when all who are in the tombs will hear his voice [29] and come forth, those who have done good, to the resurrection of life, and those who have done evil, to the resurrection of judgment.

Third Sunday in Lent

Life or judgment, the choice is ours to make.

Revelation 21:9-27

9 *Then came one of the seven angels who had the seven bowls full of the seven last plagues, and spoke to me, saying, "Come, I will show you the Bride, the wife of the Lamb." ¹⁰ And in the Spirit he carried me away to a great, high mountain, and showed me the holy city of Jerusalem coming down out of heaven from God, ¹¹ having the glory of God, its radiance like a most rare jewel, like a jasper, clear as crystal ¹² It had a great, high wall, with twelve gates, and at the gates twelve angels, and on the gates the names of the twelve tribes of the sons of Israel were inscribed; ¹³ on the east three gates, on the north three gates, on the south three gates, and on the west three gates. ¹⁴ And the wall of the city had twelve foundations, and on them the twelve names of the twelve apostles of the lamb.*

15 *And he who talked to me had a measuring rod of gold to measure the city and its gates and walls. ¹⁶ The city lies foursquare, its length the same as its breadth; and he measured the city with his rod, twelve thousand stadia; its length and breadth and height are equal. ¹⁷ He also measured its wall, a hundred and forty-four cubits by a man's measure, that is, an angel's. ¹⁸ The wall was built of jasper, while the city pure gold, clear as glass. ¹⁹ The foundations of the wall of the city were adorned with every jewel; the first was jasper, the second sapphire, the third agate, the fourth emerald, ²⁰ the fifth onyx, the sixth carnelian, the seventh chrysolite, the eighth beryl, the ninth topaz, the tenth chrsoprase, the eleventh jacinth, the twelfth amethyst. ²¹ And the twelve gates were twelve pearls, each of the gates made of a single pearl, and the street of the city was pure gold, transparent as glass.*

22 *And I saw no temple in the city, for its temple is the Lord God the Almighty and the Lamb.* ²³ *And the city has no need of sun or moon to shine upon it, for the glory of God is its light, and its lamp is the Lamb.* ²⁴ *By its light shall the nations walk; and the kings of the earth shall bring their glory into it,* ²⁵ *and its gates shall never be shut by day—and there shall be no night there;* ²⁶ *they shall bring into it the glory and the honor of the nations* ²⁷ *But nothing unclean shall enter it, nor any one who practices abomination or falsehood, but only those who are written in the Lamb's book of life.*

Day 17, Monday—Book of Life

Food for Thought

As humans we can only try to visualize the description of the new Jerusalem that John has given us in this passage. It is more than we could ever possibly imagine. The beauty of gems will be breathtaking. There will be nothing that can even compare to this new Jerusalem. The Lord Himself will be the temple there and it will be His glory that radiates to produce all the light that is needed. There will not be any problems there or any sickness. Nothing unclean will ever enter through the gates of pearl. Just imagine a pearl so big it can make an entire gate.

This is the place that has been promised to all who believe in Jesus Christ as Savior and Lord. Is your name written in the Lamb's book of life?

Prayer

Dear Heavenly Father, You have given us such a beautiful picture of the new Jerusalem through Your servant John. I thank You for a glimpse of what we have in store when the worries of this passing life are over. Thank you for Your promise of eternal life through Your Son, Jesus Christ.

Amen

Philippians 4:4-7

4 Rejoice in the Lord always; again I will say, Rejoice. 5 Let all men know your forbearance. The Lord is at hand. 6 Have no anxiety about anything, but in everything by prayer and supplication with thanksgiving let your requests be made known to God. 7 And the peace of God, which passes all understanding, will keep your hearts and your minds in Christ Jesus.

Day 18, Tuesday — Just Ask

Food for Thought

"I asked the Lord to comfort me when things weren't going my way. He said to me, 'I will comfort you, and lift your cares away.' I asked the Lord to walk with me when darkness was all that I knew. He said to me, 'Never be afraid, for I will see you through.'"

"I didn't ask for riches, He gave me wealth untold. The moon, the stars, the sun, the sky, He gave me eyes to behold. I thank the Lord for everything and I count my blessings each day. He came to me when I needed Him, I only had to pray. He'll come to you if you ask Him to, He's only a Prayer away."

These lyrics written by Johnny Lange and Jimmy Duncan, state so simply how all we need to do is pray and God will be there for our every need. It is so simple, yet oftentimes so hard to let go and really give our cares to Him.

Prayer

Lord, Help me to remember that all I need to do is pray and You will be there. Help me to always look to You for comfort and to thank You daily for my many blessings.

Amen

2 Timothy 2:14-16

14 Remind them of this, and charge them before the Lord to avoid disputing about works, which does no good, but only ruins the hearers. [15] Do your best to present yourself to God as one approved, a workman who has no need to be ashamed, rightly handling the word of truth. [16] Avoid such godless chatter, for it will lead people into more and more ungodliness.

Day 19, Wednesday — A Top Seller

Food for Thought

Just plug it in and push a button. What an age of technology we live in! Brilliant minds have invented so many wonderful inventions.

There is no doubt that the computer is here to stay. With the passing of each year it will only advance more and be able to do more things. One of the latest new developments is an electronic pocket Bible. It is compact and even has a topical word index. This was developed because the Bible is still one of the top sellers. All these years have passed and still the Word of God is a hot item. It comes in different versions, in different languages, with or without "helps," in paperback or leather bound. The Word of God is a best seller.

Read it daily and grow close to Him. Know the Word of God from cover to cover that you may show yourself as one who knows The Word. Entrust His Word with others and share His life with them.

Prayer

Dear Heavenly Father, how precious is Your Word. Like a nugget of gold it gleams forth truths to those who take the time to read it. Thank You for giving us a top seller.

Amen

Hebrews 11:1-3

1 Now faith is the assurance of things hoped for, the conviction of things not seen. ²For by it the men of old received divine approval ³By faith we understand that the world was created by the word of God, so that what is seen was made out of things which do not appear.

Day 20, Thursday —
Faith = Belief Without Question

Food for Thought

The dictionary meaning of faith is: "belief or trust that does not question or ask for proof." As a Christian we are told to have faith in God. We are to believe in Him even though we cannot see Him.

There are many who put their faith in tangible items. They have faith in the security of a job or the wealth and beauty of a home; they have faith in the closeness of a family. What happens when all this crumbles—a job is lost, a home destroyed, or divorce breaks up the family. Their faith is lost and for some it is at those times when they reach out in faith toward God for a hand to save them. They realize the tangibles are gone and they must believe in someone they cannot even see. For many it is hard to believe in something you cannot see.

We may not be able to see God, but if your faith is strong you can certainly feel His presence. He will take care of you if you let Him. He will answer your prayers if you really lift them up to Him.

God may not be able to be seen, but He can be very, very real. Feel His presence with you today.

Prayer

Dear Lord, we often tend to doubt and we often want proof of Your existence. Help us Lord to believe and to know that Your presence is very real. Help me through faith to give all my cares to You.

Amen

Romans 5:1-5

1 Therefore, since we are justified by faith, we have peace with God through our Lord Jesus Christ. ² Through him we have obtained access to this grace in which we stand, and we rejoice in our hope of sharing the glory of God. ³ More than that, we rejoice in our sufferings, knowing that suffering produces endurance, ⁴ and endurance produces character, and character produces hope, ⁵ and hope does not disappoint us, because God's love has been poured into our hearts through the Holy Spirit which has been given to us.

Day 21, Friday — Contagious Love

Food for Thought

When was the last time you felt contagious love? Have you ever been to a revival or in a room filled with Christians singing the doxology? Have you been to a Bible study when the love and caring were poured out upon one who was hurting? Have you been in a small group where you could share your deepest thoughts and know you were secure doing it?

It is within these places that you can find contagious love. It is love that spreads like fire from person to person through smiling, caring, holding hands and praying, and through hugs. It is the warmth that makes you feel comfort and safe.

If you have never experienced this contagious love, start looking for it. It is a wonderful experience that you will never regret. Where there is Christ and the Spirit you will feel His contagious love.

Prayer

Lord, You are the giver of all love. Through You spreads a love that is extremely contagious. Help me to spread Your contagious love to those around me.

Amen

Hebrews 13:8-9

8 Jesus Christ is the same yesterday and today and for ever. ⁹ Do not be led away by diverse and strange teachings; for it is well that the heart be strengthened by grace, not by foods, which have not benefited their adherents.

Day 22, Saturday —
Christ is Consistent

Food for Thought

There is not much in this world that is consistent. Things change so rapidly. Our lives are constantly being juggled around with one thing or another. Relationships no longer are given much chance to become consistent. Schooling for children is constantly changing with new technology.

Children need consistency in their lives. They need parents who are consistent in their love and in their discipline. They need the consistency of schedules and responsibilities.

There is one whom we can always count on to be true to His Word and consistent. That is Jesus Christ. "He is the same yesterday, today and forever." He is always there. We do not have to worry whether He is having a good day or a bad one. He will be there for us if we just ask.

Practice showing consistency in your life and to those around you. Count on Christ to always be there and He will not let you down.

Prayer

Dear Lord, in a world that is so full of change, I am so thankful that You remain the same. Help me to keep You a constant in my life.

Amen

John 6:27-40

27 "Do not labor for the food which perishes, but for the food which endures to eternal life, which the Son of man will give to you; for on him has God the Father set his seal." [28] Then they said to him, "What must we do, to be doing the work of God?" [29] Jesus answered them, "This is the work of God, that you believe in him whom he has sent." [30] So they said to him, "Then what sign do you do, that we may see, and believe you? What work do you perform? [31] Our fathers ate the manna in the wilderness; as it is written, 'He gave them bread from heaven to eat.'" [32] Jesus then said to them, "Truly, truly I say to you, it was not Moses who gave you the bread from heaven; my Father gives you the true bread from heaven. [33] For the bread of God is that which comes down from heaven, and gives life to the world." [34] They said to him, "Lord, give us this bread always."

35 Jesus said to them, "I am the bread of life; he who comes to me shall not hunger, and he who believes in me shall never thirst. [36] But I said to you that you have seen me and yet do not believe. [37] All that the Father gives me will come to me; and him who comes to me I will not cast out. [38] for I have come down from heaven, not to do my own will, but the will of him who sent me. [39] and this is the will of him who sent me, that I should lose nothing of all that he has given me, but raise it up at the last day. [40] For this is the will of my Father, that every one who sees the Son and believes in him should have eternal life; and I will raise him up at the last day."

Fourth Sunday in Lent

We need not hunger or thirst if we believe in Him.

Ephesians 6:10-17

10 *Finally, be strong in the Lord and in the strength of his might.* ¹¹ *Put on the whole armor of God, that you may be able to stand against the wiles of the devil.* ¹² *For we are not contending against flesh and blood, but against the principalities, against the powers, against the world rulers of this present darkness, against the spiritual hosts of wickedness in the heavenly places.* ¹³ *Therefore take the whole armor of God, that you may be able to withstand in the evil day, and having done all, to stand.* ¹⁴ *Stand therefore, having girded your loins with truth, and having put on the breastplate of righteousness,* ¹⁵ *and having shod your feet with the equipment of the gospel of peace;* ¹⁶ *above all taking the shield of faith, with which you can quench all the flaming darts of the evil one.* ¹⁷ *And take the helmet of salvation, and the sword of the Spirit, which is the word of God.*

Day 23, Monday — Armor Yourself

Food for Thought

As a Christian we need to put on the whole armor of God. We need to be filled with the knowledge of His Word so we can withstand the attacks of Satan.

Fill your life with things from above and keep focused on them. Do not allow any room in your heart for Satan to sneak in. Satan is very clever in his attacks, so clever we do not always see him. Be alert to his every move so that your guard will not be down.

If we keep our focus on Christ, we will become more like Him. We can develop the traits that come from above: holiness, compassion, kindness, lowliness, meekness, patience, forgiveness, but most of all, love.

Prayer

Dear Jesus, help me to focus only on You and the qualities that I can develop from above. Help me to be aware of the many ways Satan will try to attack and to turn away from what is earthly in me.

Amen

James 1:2-4

2 Count it all joy, my brethren, when you meet various trials, ³ for you know that the testing of your faith produces steadfastness. ⁴ And let steadfastness have its full effect, that you may be perfect and complete, lacking in nothing.

Day 24, Tuesday—
It's Not an Umbrella Policy

Food for Thought

Christianity is not an umbrella policy. It does not prevent things from going wrong. It can make things much easier to handle when things do get tough.

Sometimes people think that once they become a Christian that God will protect them from bad things that happen. Christianity does not do that for us. Life still happens. Sometimes there is death, sickness, financial difficulties, and all the other pains associated with life. Christianity gives us a buffer, a hope, and a promise. It helps us get through the tough times and it gives us someone to turn to for comfort and answers.

Prayer

Dear Lord, Each person is faced with hard times in life in varying degrees. Help me to know that being Christian will not shield me from those times, yet it will make it much easier to get through them.

Amen

James 4:13-17

13 Come now, you who say, "Today or tomorrow we will go into such and such a town and spend a year there and trade and get gain" [14] whereas you do not know about tomorrow. What is your life? For you are a mist that appears for a little time and then vanishes. [15] Instead you ought to say, "If the Lord wills, we shall live and we shall do this or that." [16] As it is, you boast in your arrogance. All such boasting is evil. [17] Whoever knows what is right is right to do and fails to do it, for him it is sin.

Day 25, Wednesday —
Just a Speck in Time

Food for Thought

This world is just a temporary home. This life we live is merely a speck in time. Spending time gathering up earthly possessions is a waste of time. These things will not be needed in eternity, so focus on what you can take with you.

How many times have you helped a friend in need? How many prayers have you lifted up for those who are hurting? How about the warmth and the love you gave someone through a hug, or the handkerchief you lent someone to wipe away a tear? Remember the meal you prepared for someone just out of the hospital? Think of the laughter you share with your family during a meal.

I hope your life contains many of these precious memories. For it is in giving that we receive. It is the many we have cared for, loved and shared God's love with that we will take to eternity.

Make sure you know where those you love and yourself will spend eternity!

Prayer

Lord, You are the giver of life and it is a wonderful gift. Help us to remember the importance of what really matters in this life. Help us not to focus on earthly possessions that will be meaningless in eternity.

Amen

John 3:16-21

16 For God so loved the world that he gave his only Son, that whoever believes in him should not perish but have eternal life. [17] For God sent the Son into the world, not to condemn the world, but that the world might be saved through him. [18] He who believes in him is not condemned; he who does not believe is condemned already, because he has not believed in the name of the only Son of God. [19] And this is the judgment, that the light has come into the world, and men loved darkness rather than light, because their deeds were evil. [20] For every one who does evil hates the light, and does not come to the light, lest his deeds should be exposed. [21] But he who does what is true comes to the light, that it may be clearly seen that his deeds have been wrought in God.

Day 26, Thursday — Love

Food for Thought

This passage in Scripture contains one of the most well-known verses in the Bible. It is one many have memorized, underlined and put stars and hearts by in their Bibles.

This passage tells of the kind of love that God has for us. The love that He has shows giving and not taking. The love talked about here is a verb; it is an action word that shows the tremendous impact of God's love.

God gave His only Son for each one of us. What greater expression of love could He ever have done for us? There is none. He did the ultimate in love for us.

What kind of a lover are you? Is your love a verb? Are you giving rather than taking? Strive to make your love a God-like love.

Prayer

Lord, I come to you today asking that I might learn to love in a God-like way. Help me to give to those around me and let Your love shine through me.

Amen

Matthew 7:7-12

7 "Ask, and it will be given to you; seek, and you shall find; knock, and it will be opened to you. ⁸ For every one who asks receives, and he who seeks finds, and to him who knocks it will be opened. ⁹ Or what man of you, if his son asks him for bread, will give him a stone? ¹⁰ Or if he asks for a fish, will give him a serpent: ¹¹ If you then, who are evil, know how to give good gifts to your children, how much more will your Father who is in heaven give good things to those who ask him! ¹² So whatever you wish that men would do to you, do so to them; for this is the law and the prophets.

Day 27, Friday — Ask, Seek, and Knock

Food for Thought

Which door will it be? Door number 1, door number 2, or door number 3? Sometimes our lives are like this. We face circumstances we are unsure of. We face a future that is uncertain and we are not quite sure which way to turn.

God's Word tells us to "ask and it will be given, seek and you will find, knock and it will be opened to you." It may be that what we ask for is answered in a different way than what we wanted. It may be that what we are looking for shows up in the place we least expected. It also could be that the door we chose to knock on was the wrong door and we might have to go to another one.

Make sure your life is in tune to Christ when you ask, seek and knock. Make sure you listen to Him if you are going to ask Him.

God has many ways of showing us the right door to knock on. Listen to those Christian friends that you encounter, listen to Christian messages that might be God talking to you. Most important of all is to stay in constant communication with God. He is always there, waiting.

Prayer

Dear Lord, I find myself in times of uncertainties sometimes wanting to throw in the towel, then I realize that this is not the answer. You have the answers for me. Help me to ask, seek and knock on Your door every day.

Amen

Matthew 6:25-34

25 "Therefore I tell you, do not be anxious about your life, what you shall eat or what you shall drink, nor about your body, what you shall put on. Is not life more than food, and the body more than clothing? [26] Look at the birds of the air: they neither sow nor reap nor gather into barns, and yet your heavenly Father feeds them. Are you not of more value than they? [27] And which of you by being anxious can add one cubit to his span of life? [28] And why are you anxious about clothing? Consider the lilies of the field, how they grow; they neither toil nor spin; [29] yet I tell you, even Solomon in all his glory was not arrayed like one of these. [30] But if God so clothes the grass of the field, which today is alive and tomorrow is thrown into the oven, will he not much more clothe you, O men of little faith: [31] Therefore do not be anxious, saying, 'What shall we eat?' or 'What shall we drink?' or 'What shall we wear?' [32] For the Gentiles seek all these things; and your heavenly Father knows that you need them all. [33] But seek first his kingdom and his righteousness, and all these things shall be yours as well.

34 "Therefore do not be anxious about tomorrow, for tomorrow will be anxious for itself. Let the day's own trouble be sufficient for the day.

Day 28, Saturday—Borrowed Trouble

Food for Thought

How many times does our life take a turn and leave us wondering what will happen next? God's Word tells us "not to be anxious about tomorrow, it will take care of itself."

So often we tend to worry about what tomorrow will bring. We borrow trouble as if we do not have enough for one day. God knows our every need. He will take care of us. We need to seek the will of God and concentrate on doing what is right and good. This does not give us, as Christians, an excuse to be lazy, but merely shows us that there are very important things we need to do with our time. Use your time wisely; do not borrow trouble.

Prayer

Lord, how often we forget of Your magnificent power and strength. We always try to do things on our own. Help us to give to You the petty worries that fill so much of our time. Help us to use our time for greater things.

Amen

John 8:46-59

46 *"Which of you convicts me of sin? If I tell the truth, why do you not believe me?* ⁴⁷ *He who is of God hears the words of God; the reason why you do not hear them is that you are not of God."*

48 *The Jews answered him, "Are we not right in saying that you are a Samaritan and have a demon?"* ⁴⁹ *Jesus answered, "I have not a demon; but I honor my Father, and you dishonor me.* ⁵⁰ *Yet I do not seek my own glory; there is One who seeks it and he will be the judge.* ⁵¹ *Truly, truly, I say to you, if any one keeps my word, he will never see death."*

52 *The Jews said to him, "Now we know that you have a demon. Abraham died, as did the prophets; and you say, "If any one keeps my word, he will never taste death."* ⁵³ *Are you greater than our father Abraham, who died: And the prophets died! Who do you claim to be?"* ⁵⁴ *Jesus answered, "If I glorify myself, my glory is nothing; it is my Father who glorifies me, of whom, you say that he is your God.* ⁵⁵ *But you have not known him; I know him. If I said, I do not know him, I should be a liar like you; but I do know him and I keep his word.* ⁵⁶ *Your father Abraham rejoiced that he was to see my day; he saw it and was glad."* ⁵⁷ *The Jews then said to him, "You are not yet fifty years old, and have you seen Abraham?"* ⁵⁸ *Jesus said to them, "Truly, truly, I say to you, before Abraham was, I am."* ⁵⁹ *So they took up stones to throw at him; but Jesus hid himself, and went out of the temple.*

Fifth Sunday in Lent

Hear the Word, keep the Word and glorify God.

Psalm 28

A Psalm of David
1 To thee, O Lord, I call
    my rock, be not deaf to me,
    lest, if thou be silent to me,
    I become like those who go down
    to the Pit.

2 Hear the voice of my supplication,
    as I cry to thee for help,
    as I lift up my hands
    toward thy most holy sanctuary.

3 Take me not off with the wicked,
    with those who are workers of evil,
    who speak peace with their neighbors,
    while mischief is in their hearts.

4 Requite them according to their work,
    and according to the evil of their deeds;
    requite them according to the work
    of their hands;
    render them their due award.

5 Because they do not regard the works of the Lord,
    or the work of his hands,
    he will break them down and build them up no more.

6 Blessed be the Lord!
    for he has heard the voice of my supplications.

7 The Lord is my strength and my shield;
    in him my heart trusts;
    so I am helped, and my heart exults,
    and with my song I give thanks to him.

8 The Lord is the strength of his people,
  he is the saving refuge of his anointed.

9 O save thy people, and bless thy heritage;
  be thou their shepherd, and carry them forever.

Day 29, Monday — Mountain Climbing

Food for Thought

Have you been mountain climbing lately? Let your life represent a mountain. Picture one of the highest mountains with an extremely difficult face to climb.

As you begin to climb the mountain it is fairly simple at the beginning. It is not real steep and it does not take intense climbing skills to get up a little ways. Now we are getting pretty sure of ourselves and the climb seems fairly easy. We begin to think we are pretty good and that we do not need the intense training that some skilled mountain climbers go through.

Suddenly the rock under your foot gives way and you grab the side of the mountain and hang on to the jagged edges. Your heart is beating hard and you start to think twice about the lessons you did not take. You might even lift up a prayer for safety since the climbing has suddenly become a little tougher.

A short time passes and you muster up your courage and begin to climb again. This is a harder part of the mountain and you have to go much slower. Once again you become sure of yourself one more time. You tend to forget about that prayer you said a while ago and you take it for granted that you are doing this climbing on your own. Then, another slip, this one much worse than the first and once again you pray for skill and safety.

This story could continue and each one of us could have different results. We might make it to the top and if we do, what will our reaction be? Will it be one of praise and thanksgiving, or will we pat ourselves on the back and say what a wonderful climber we have become?

This experience is not limited only to mountain climbing. In our daily lives we ask God for help, and when He gives it, do we always remember to thank Him? Sometimes we get pretty sure of ourselves until we slip again. Do not forget who is helping you!

Prayer

Lord, we all have mountains in our lives. Some are much steeper than others. Some places become so hard that we are not sure how we can possibly make it. Thank You that we can come to You for help and You are always there. Help me to remember who it is that is helping me.

Amen

Hebrews 10:26-31

26 For if we sin deliberately after receiving the knowledge of the truth,
there no longer remains a sacrifice for sins, 27 but a fearful prospect of
judgement, and a fury of fire which will consume the adversaries.
28 A man who has violated the law of Moses dies without mercy at the
testimony of two or three witnesses. 29 How much worse punishment
do you think will be deserved by the man who has spurned the Son
of God, and profaned the blood of the covenant by which he was
sanctified, and outraged the Spirit of grace? 30 For we know him who
said, "Vengeance is mine, I will repay." And again, "The Lord will
judge his people." 31 It is a fearful thing to fall into the hands of the
living God.

Day 30, Tuesday — God's Grace

Food for Thought

We hear a lot about God's grace today. His grace is a marvelous gift to us. However, we need to be careful that we do not use God's grace to excuse our actions. We need to make sure we do not justify our sinning because of God's grace. Have you ever done something you know is wrong but you justified it because you knew God would forgive you anyway?

As a Christian we should never take advantage of such a marvelous gift. Don't use God's grace as a scapegoat for your actions. For the "Lord will judge His people."

Prayer

Lord, forgive me for the times I have abused Your grace. Help me to see the beauty of Your grace as well as its intended purpose.

Amen

Luke 9:23-27

23 And he said to all, "If any man would come after me, let him deny himself and take up his cross daily and follow me. 24 For whoever would save his life will lose it; and whoever loses his life for my sake, he will save it. 25 For what does it profit a man if he gains the whole world and loses or forfeits himself? 26 For whoever is ashamed of me and of my words, of him will the Son of man be ashamed when he comes in his glory and the glory of the Father and of the holy angels. 27 But I tell you truly, there are some standing here who will not taste death before they see the kingdom of God."

Day 31, Wednesday —
Cheaper or Richer, It's Your Choice

Food for Thought

What price are you willing to pay for Christ? Do you want a cheap plastic, three-dollar Christ that you can set up on a shelf, or do you want one that you can consider from time to time that will not get in your way? Do you want a Christ that you can be happy with and then use as someone to blame when things do not go your way? Or are you willing to pay more and have the Christ who is with you every day, the Christ whom you will worship, pray to and follow all the way? Are you willing to give your life to Christ and let Him lead the way?

What kind of Christ are you looking for? Each of us must choose.

Prayer

Lord, I know the kind of Christ I want in my life. I am willing to give You my life for Your service every day.

Amen

Psalm 25:4-10

4 Make me to know thy ways, O Lord;
　　teach me thy paths.
5 Lead me in thy truth, and teach me,
　　for thou art the God of my salvation;
　　for thee I wait all the day long.

6 Be mindful of thy mercy, O Lord,
　　and of thy steadfast love,
　　for they have been from of old,
7 Remember not the sins of my youth,
　　or my transgressions;
　　according to thy steadfast love remember me,
　　for thy goodness' sake, O Lord!

8 Good and upright is the Lord;
　　therefore he instructs sinners in the way.
9 He leads the humble in what is right,
　　and teaches the humble his way.
10 All the paths of the Lord are steadfast love and faithfulness,
　　for those who keep his covenant and his testimonies.

Day 32, Thursday — A Guided Tour

Food for Thought

Is your life a reflection of God's love? Does your home reflect His beauty? How often do you dust your Bible, or is it well-read every day? If God were to go away how long would it be before you noticed He was gone?

As a Christian our lives need to be focused on Christ. He needs to be out constant guide. He needs to be so close that if He left for just a minute you would feel an emptiness inside.

Do not let your Bible get dusty. Do not allow God to leave your side. Stay with Him constantly. He will be your guide.

Prayer

Lord, I desire this guided tour of life that only You can take me on. Help me to follow where You lead.

Amen

Philippians 1:3-6

3 I thank my God in all my remembrance of you, ⁴ always in every
prayer of mine for you all making my prayer with joy, ⁵ thankful for
your partnership in the gospel from the first day until now. ⁶ And I
am sure that he who began a good work in you will bring it to com-
pletion at the day of Jesus Christ.

Day 33, Friday — God is not Finished Yet!

Food for Thought

We are over halfway through our Lenten journey. Holy week will soon be upon us. Having spent thirty-three days in a routine of Bible reading and prayer should be long enough to have formed a habit. As tender loving jewels I pray that chips have been made in some of the rough edges and they have created more sparkle and shine in your life.

Each one of us will always have rough edges to work on. I am grateful that God's Word assures us that God is not finished with us yet. He will continue to help us grow and shine until "the day of Jesus Christ."

Prayer

Lord, I am so grateful to know that You will always be working on me. Mold me and make me a very special jewel for Your service.

Amen

John 13:1-11

1 *Now before the feast of the Passover, when Jesus knew that his hour had come to depart out of this world to the Father, having loved his own who were in the world, he loved them to the end.* ² *And during supper, when the devil had already put it into the heart of Judas Iscariot, Simon's son, to betray him,* ³ *Jesus, knowing that the Father had given all things into his hands, and that he had come from God and was going to God,* ⁴ *rose from supper, laid aside his garments, and girded himself with a towel.* ⁵ *Then he poured water into a basin, and began to wish the disciples' feet, and to wipe them with the towel with which he was girded.* ⁶ *He came to Simon Peter; and Peter said to him, "Lord, do you wash my feet:"* ⁷ *Jesus answered him, "What I am doing you do not know now, but afterward you will understand."* ⁸ *Peter said to him, "You shall never wash my feet." Jesus answered him, "If I do not wash you, you have no part in me."* ⁹ *Simon Peter said to him, "Lord, not my feet only but also my hands and my head!"* ¹⁰ *Jesus said to him, "He who has bathed does not need to wash, except for his feet, but he is clean all over; and you are clean, but not all of you.* ¹¹ *For he knew who was to betray him; that was why he said, "You are not all clean."*

Day 34, Saturday—
Take a Walk with God

Food for Thought

Just before Holy Week is upon us let Jesus take you on a walk. If you can't visualize it then actually take a physical walk. Make sure Jesus is with you. Let Him take you on this walk.

Experience with Him what He felt and was about to encounter before facing His death. Feel His warmth as you hold His hand before it was pierced. Remember that Jesus was human and experienced human emotions. He has hurt just as we have and then some. He has wept tears of joy and of sorrow just as we have.

Imagine how anxious He must have been, knowing this was His last week as a man. He knew He had a future with the Father, yet He must have wondered if He would really have to endure such pain. As He met with the disciples at the Last Supper, Jesus gave them all a special gift. He knelt down to wash their feet, one by one. He wanted them to know of His love for them and to see His servant nature. He wanted them to know all that was to happen and that He would be with them again.

Jesus the Son was crucified like a common criminal. Unlike any other He rose again so we might have life and have it so abundantly.

Prayer

Dear Jesus, I can only imagine the fear of facing that cross, yet You did it to save all of us who are lost. A simple thank you is hardly enough to repay You for the ultimate sacrifice. I accept Your love and in return I give You my life in servitude.

Amen

Luke 19:41-48

41 And when he drew near and saw the city he wept over it, ⁴²saying, "Would that even today you knew the things that make for peace! But now they are hid from your eyes. ⁴³For the days shall come upon you, when your enemies will cast up a bank about you and surround you, and hem you in on every side, ⁴⁴and dash you to the ground, you and your children within you, and they will not leave one stone upon another in you; because you did not know the time of your visitation."

45 And he entered the temple and began to drive out those who sold, ⁴⁶saying to them, "It is written, 'My house shall be a house of prayer'; but you have made it a den of robbers."

47 And he was teaching daily in the temple. The chief priests and the scribes and the principal men of the people sought to destroy him; ⁴⁸but they did not find anything they could do, for all the people hung upon his words.

Sixth Sunday in Lent

Is Christ weeping over your life?

Psalm 90:1-12

1 Lord, thou hast been our dwelling place in all generations.

2 Before the mountains were brought forth,
   or ever thou hadst formed the earth and the world,
   from everlasting to everlasting thou art God.

3 Thou turnest man back to the dust,
   and sayest, "Turn back, O children of men!"

4 For a thousand years in thy sight are but as yesterday when it is past,
   or as a watch in the night.

5 Thou dost sweep men away; they are like a dream,
   like grass which is renewed in the morning:

6 in the morning it flourishes and is renewed;
   in the evening it fades and withers.

7 For we are consumed by thy anger;
   by thy wrath we are overwhelmed.

8 Thou hast set our iniquities before thee,
   our secret sins in the light of thy countenance.

9 For all our days pass away under thy wrath,
   our years come to an end like a sigh.

10 The years of our life are threescore and ten
   or even by reason of strength fourscore;
   yet their span is but toil and trouble;
   they are soon gone, and we fly away.

11 Who considers the power of thy anger,
   and thy wrath according to the fear of thee?

12 So teach us to number our days
   that we may get a heart of wisdom.

Day 35, Monday of Holy Week — Fragile, Handle with Care

Food for Thought

Life. Such a precious gift, yet so fragile that in moments it can be shattered.

Why do we wait for disaster to strike before we wake up and notice just how fragile life can be? For some, life is short. For some it is in between. We never know for any of us how long life will be.

"So take each moment, and live each moment, in peace eternally. Let there be peace on earth, and let it begin with me."

Prayer

Dear God, may I take my life and live it to the fullest.
Help me not to take advantage of such a precious gift. Let
me live each moment in peace and for Your glory.

Amen

John 14:1-14

1 "Let not your hearts be troubled; believe in God, believe also in me.
  ² In my Father's house are many rooms; if it were not so, would I
  have told you that I go to prepare a place for you? ³ And when I go
  and prepare a place for you, I will come again and will take you to
  myself, that where I am you may be also. ⁴ And you know the way
  where I am going." ⁵ Thomas said to him, "Lord, we do not know
  where you are going; how can we know the way?" ⁶ Jesus said to
  him, "I am the way, and the truth, and the life, no one comes to the
  Father, but by me. ⁷ If you had known me, you would have known
  my Father also; henceforth you know him and have seen him."

8 Philip said to him, "Lord, show us the Father, and we shall be satisfied." ⁹ Jesus said to him, "Have I been with you so long, and yet you
  do not know me, Philip? He who has seen me has seen the Father;
  how can you say, 'Show us the Father?' ¹⁰ Do you not believe that I
  am in the Father and the Father in me? The words that I say to you I
  do not speak on my own authority; but the Father who dwells in me
  does his works. ¹¹ Believe me that I am in the Father and the Father in
  me; or else believe me for the sake of the works themselves.

12 "Truly, truly, I say to you, he who believes in me will also do the
  works that I do; and greater works than these will he do, because I go
  to the Father. ¹³ Whatever you ask in my name, I will do it, that the
  Father may be glorified in the Son; ¹⁴ if you ask anything in my
  name, I will do it."

Day 36, Tuesday in Holy Week — Focus on Life Rather Than Suffering

Food for Thought

Jesus was facing death on the cross, but He didn't focus on His death. He was focused on the feelings of those around Him. He was concerned that the disciples would be troubled with His leaving. He took the time to explain to them that where He was going they would someday be also. As they questioned Him, He took the time to explain how He and the Father are one. He promised that whatever would be asked in His name He would do it.

Jesus did not focus on His suffering that He would endure, but rather on the life that we could have through His life. In all suffering there can be joy if we do not focus on the pain.

Prayer

Dear Jesus, such wonderful lessons we can learn from Your Word. Help us in the midst of suffering to be able to see past the pain so that in joy we can help others.

Amen

John 16:32-33, 17:1-5

32 *The hour is coming, indeed it has come, when you will be scattered, every man to his home, and will leave me alone; yet I am not alone, for the Father is with me.* [33] *I have said this to you, that in me you may have peace. In the world you have tribulation; but be of good cheer, I have overcome the world."*

* * *

1 *When Jesus had spoken these works, he lifted up his eyes to heaven and said, "Father, the hour has come; glorify thy Son that the Son may glorify thee,* [2] *since thou hast given him power over all flesh, to give eternal life to all whom thou hast given him.* [3] *And this is eternal life, that they know thee the only true God, and Jesus Christ whom thou hast sent.*

4 *I glorified thee on earth, having accomplished the work which thou gavest to me to do;* [5] *and now, Father, glorify thou me in thy own presence with the glory which I had with thee before the world was made.*

Day 37, Wednesday of Holy Week — Peace in the Midst of Strife

Food for Thought

In the midst of such great tribulation we are able to have peace. In the midst of suffering and pain we can still be optimistic.

Jesus' work was finished. He was now going to go back home, to be with His Father. We can rejoice in knowing that His suffering would soon be over and that He would be home again. What a wonderful gift for us His life was. If we love Christ we can overcome the strife of life and have peace because nothing is too hard for Christ to endure, and in Christ we can have peace.

Prayer

Lord Jesus, You were prepared to bear the cross. You prepared Your disciples for what would happen. You have given us hope and peace through Your Son, Jesus Christ, even in the midst of strife.

Amen

John 19:23-30

23 When the soldiers had crucified Jesus they took his garments and made four parts, one for each soldier; also his tunic. But the tunic was without seam, woven from top to bottom; 24 so they said to one another, "Let us not tear it, but cast lots for it to see whose it shall be." This was to fulfil the scripture,
"They parted my garments among them,
and for my clothing they cast lots."

25 So the soldiers did this. But standing by the cross of Jesus were his mother, and his mother's sister, Mary the wife of Clopas, and Mary Magdalene. 26 When Jesus saw his mother, and the disciple whom he loved standing near, he said to his mother, "Woman, behold your son!" 27 Then he said to the disciple, "Behold, your mother!" And from that hour the disciple took her to his own home.

28 After this Jesus, knowing that all was now finished, said (to fulfil the scripture), "I thirst." 29 A bowl full of vinegar stood there; to they put a sponge full of the vinegar on hyssop and held it to his mouth. 30 When Jesus had received the vinegar, he said, "It is finished"; and he bowed his head and gave up his spirit.

Day 38, Maundy-Thursday — The End

Food for Thought

I remember standing in a line at a discount store just chatting with a friend. I noticed an older fellow behind me, also waiting patiently for his turn at the checkout. Then the next thing I remember was being lost and I could not find my friend. I wanted to call out to her, but everything was going dim. Then darkness overcame me, and I was in a tunnel with no end. The tunnel was so long and dark I could see only a speck of light at the other end. Then the light started getting brighter. I thought I must be getting closer to the end. Then I remembered I had heard of such a tunnel, but it was from people who had seen the end. I looked both ways. I wanted to turn back. I wanted to find my family and friends.

"God," I called, "You have made a mistake. You probably wanted that older man. I have a family. They are still young. Who will take care of them if I am gone? Who will take care of the schedules and all the different things to do? What about my parents, my sisters and brothers, my friends? They will be hurt and they too will question, 'Why Lord, why?'

"The light is getting so bright, Lord. Couldn't I do more to help You by sharing Your love on this earth? I thought I would have so much time to do all those things I promised I would. I did not expect my life to be so short. I did not expect the end."

We never expect the end and we always put off many of the most important things in life. Share today the life of Christ with a friend. For Christ, His death was not the end but He too was very young. He knew that He must die to give new life to His friends. For us death also is reality, but we do not know when. Will you be ready or will you keep expecting more time to do what is important and to keep all the promises you have made to God and your friends?

Prayer

Dear Lord, forgive me for acting like I will always have tomorrow. Help me to do what is important. Help me to share the promises of Your Word with a friend.

Amen

John 11:28-44

28 When she had said this, she went and called her sister Mary, saying quietly, "The Teacher is here and is calling for you." 29 And when she heard it, she rose quickly and went to him. 30 Now Jesus had not yet come to the village, but was still in the place where Martha had met him. 31 When the Jews who were with her in the house, consoling her, saw Mary rise quickly and go out, they followed her, supposing that she was going to the tomb to weep there. 32 Then Mary, when she came where Jesus was and saw him, fell at his feet, saying to him, "Lord, if you had been here, my brother would not have died." 33 When Jesus saw her weeping, and the Jews who came with her also weeping, he was deeply moved in spirit and troubled; 34 and he said, "Where have you laid him?" They said to him, "Lord, come and see." 35 Jesus wept. 36 So the Jews said, "See how he loved him!" 37 But some of them said, "Could not be who opened the eyes of the blind man have kept this man from dying?"

38 Then Jesus, deeply moved again, came to the tomb; it was a cave, and a stone lay upon it. 39 Jesus said, "Take away the stone." Martha, the sister of the dead man, said to him, "Lord, by this time there will be an odor, for he has been dead four days." 40 Jesus said to her, "Did I not tell you that if you would believe you would see the glory of God?" 41 So they took away the stone. And Jesus lifted up his eyes and said, "Father, I thank thee that thou hast heard me. 42 I knew that thou hearest me always, but I have said this on account of the people standing by, that they may believe that thou didst send me." 43 When he had said this, he cried with a loud voice, Lazarus, come out." 44 The dead man came out, his hands and feet bound with bandages, and his face wrapped with a cloth. Jesus said to them, "Unbind him, and let him go."

Day 39, Good Friday — "Jesus Wept"

Food for Thought

This is the old familiar story of Lazarus. It contains the shortest verse in the Bible. John 11:35 says, "Jesus wept." This verse shows us Christ's compassion.

Jesus knew that Lazarus would be brought back to life. He knew the outcome, yet He felt so deeply for Mary and Martha that He wept. Jesus feels our pain and sorrow and weeps with us even though He knows the tomorrows.

Often we can be moved to tears when we think of how God gave His only Son for us. He suffered a tremendous loss so we could have life.

Despite the sorrow of Good Friday, we are assured that Christ is with us always. He is with us in our deepest sorrow and in our greatest joys.

Prayer

Lord, thank you for the assurance Your Word brings us. Thank You that You feel with us in pain and sorrow and in our joys. Thank You for the gift You have given us through Your Son, Jesus Christ.

Amen

Psalm 22:1-21

1 My God, my God, why hast thou forsaken me?
  Why art thou so far from helping me, from the words of my groaning:

2 O my God, I cry by day, but thou dost not answer;
  and by night, but find no rest.

3 Yet thou art holy, enthroned on the praises of Israel.

4 In thee our fathers trusted;
  they trusted, and thou didst deliver them.

5 To thee they cried, and were saved;
  in thee they trusted, and were not disappointed.

6 But I am a worm, and no man; scorned by men, and despised by the people.

7 All who see me mock me,
  they make mouths at me, they wag their heads;

8 "He committed his cause to the Lord; let him deliver him,
  let him rescue him, for he delights in him!"

9 Yet thou art he who took me from the womb;
  thou didst keep me safe upon my mother's breasts.

10 Upon thee was I cast from my birth,
  and since my mother bore me thou hast been my God.

11 Be not far from me,
  for trouble is near
  and there is none to help.

12 Many bulls encompass me,
  strong bulls of Bashan surround me;

13 they open wide their mouths at me,
  like a ravening and roaring lion.

14 *I am poured out like water,*
   and all my bones are out of joint;
   my heart is like wax,
   it is melted within my breast;

15 *my strength is dried up like a potsherd,*
   and my tongue cleaves to my jaws;
   thou dost lay me in the dust of death.

16 *Yea, dogs are round about me;*
   a company of evildoers encircle me;
   they have pierced my hands and feet—

17 *I can count all my bones—*
   they stare and gloat over me;

18 *they divide my garments among them,*
   and for my raiment they cast lots.

19 *But thou, O Lord, be not far off!*
   O thou my help, hasten to my aid!

20 *Deliver my soul from the sword,*
   my life from the power of the dog!

21 *Save me from the mouth of the lion,*
   my afflicted soul from the horns of the wild oxen!

Day 40, Easter Eve —
Feel His Nail Pierced Hands

Food for Thought

God's only Son was crucified. If you have ever heard the description of a crucifixion, it is very nauseating and painful just to listen to. We can only begin to imagine the pain of having nails pierced through our hands. God loves us so much that He endured the suffering of letting His only Son go through that pain.

When our children are hurt or sick it is painful to watch them suffer. It was painful to God, but he allowed it for our salvation. He gave His Son so our sins could be buried at the cross. What a sacrifice He made!

Concentrate today on making some sacrifices for God. Feel the pain of His nail pierced hands. Share the pain of someone you know who is hurting this day.

Prayer

God, help me to feel deep in my heart the sacrifice You made. Help me to bear another's pain.

Amen

1 John 1:5-10

5 The light shines in the darkness, and the darkness has not overcome it.

6 There was a man sent from God, whose name was John. ⁷ He came for testimony, to bear witness to the light, that all might believe through him. ⁸ He was not the light, but came to bear witness to the light.

9 The true light that enlightens every man was coming into the world. ¹⁰ He was in the world, and the world was made through him, yet the world knew him not.

Easter — Those Who See Light

Food for Thought

HALLELUJAH, HE HAS RISEN! What a glorious day. Christ has given us new life. Those who see Him, will walk in the light.

The Lenten Journey has ended. I hope a new life has begun.

Continue this journey with Christ daily. The words written by Rev. E. Donald Osuna in the song "Those who See Light" offer us a great Easter story.

Those who see light can walk in the dark.
Those who see love can see God.
Those who look up will discover God's face.
Those who look down will uncover God's path.
Those who perceive God is here, is with us now
Will see God's return.

Those who see light can walk in the dark.
Those who see love can see God.
Those who have witnessed the sun rise and set;
Those who have studied a flower unfold;
Those who have focused on land, sea and sky
Have seen Jesus Christ.
Those who see light can walk in the dark.
Those who see love can see God.
Those who see good in each person they meet;
Those who look after their neighbor in need;
Those who believe God's now living in them
Will see God's return.

Prayer

Lord God, We sing praises to You as we rejoice in the Risen Savior. May we look up to You, Lord, for all our needs and focus on ,so we can become more like You. Let us look to the light so we can see God.

Amen

Personal Devotions

Personal Devotions

Personal Devotions

Personal Devotions